I0467802

Stop Reset Start

Stop Reset Start

How to develop a Winning Mindset in your Team and become the Leader everyone loves to follow

Santosh Kanekar

TABLE OF CONTENTS

CHAPTER 1

Introduction

This story goes back to the early 2000s. I had just joined a Consumer Products company which was a market leader, both globally and locally. It was a world class organization, and I was truly excited to be part of the journey.

Within three months of my joining, the HR head called me and said "Son, we are glad you are here. But, we have a problem. As you know, our lead brand is declining when everyone else in the market is growing. Fix it. Now. You got three months else..."

He left the sentence incomplete, but I exactly knew what he meant. First, I was shocked and angry. I mean, I had just come in, and I had to turn around things that fast??

Next came Doubt and uncertainty. How the hell was I going to pull it off? I had a brand new team, and I was just three months in. I did not have a template which I could just copy and paste. There was no time for strategy discussions. Action had to start now. What next?

Cut to three years later, the brand was knocking the ball off the park. Everyone was gung-ho. We were ahead of our targets. Now the Board wanted more. We were egged on to take an audacious goal of doubling our volumes in next three years.

I was sitting in my hotel room while the party was going on below. I still remember looking at the beautiful PowerPoint slides and wondering what had I got myself into. Will we really pull it off? Did we have the structure and systems to deliver the plan? Did I have the right team and more importantly, the right mindset to deliver this audacious goal? Even if I did, what are the next steps? What is the exact sequence of things which need to unfold?

Have you heard this story before?

Maybe you have found yourself at this juncture sometime. Perhaps you are at this point right now. Maybe your story is different to mine, but you can relate to the events. If you are, you are not alone. And there is a way out.

The way out is not to just stumble out of the problem. But, the way out is to come out Winning.

The solution is a system. A systematic plan of building your business and your team to accelerate at will. A system to reboot the team, build the foundation and then speed up the delivery

This book will uncover the first steps for a reboot. Reboot and build a Winning Mindset.

What do we do when a car is going at high speed, and we know there is trouble in the engine? We do a Pit stop. This book is meant to be that pit stop.

We will rewire the engine for peak performance.

We will take all those actions which will bring out the high performance within you and your team. Yes within you. We have all the resources which can make us high performing. We just have to make the right adjustments in the settings to get the best out of us, today, tomorrow and all the time.

You may say "what has performance got to do with Winning Mindset"?

Countless research in sports and other high-performance situations have shown that the difference between the one at the top and rest is the Winning Mindset.

Why should you believe me?

Because I lived to tell both the tales.

No, not because I am the proverbial cat with nine lives. I had two coaches (one functional and another performance) who helped me navigate those speedboat journeys.

I had a team which truly embodied the Winning Mindset.

I was one of the few leaders who went through a Global Breakthrough Performance Coaching.

I have lived and breathed high performance in many of the Fortune 500 companies I worked in.

I advise Global Hedge Funds and VCs based in NY, London, Hong Kong and Singapore. When they want to invest in businesses and want an assessment of the management team and their ability to deliver, I am one of the people they call to get this assessment.

I help Startups in their business planning and how to accelerate their performance to enable them to get their next level of funding.

And now, I want to share all my experiences and coaching to make everyone reach their potential and beyond.

What is this Winning Mindset?

Is this mindset something one can just turn on? No

Is this a mantra which if one chants every day, one can have it? No

Can it be learned? Yes, and I am going to show how.

The Winning Mindset is made of four pillars which hold this mindset up. These four pillars ensure that once they are built and operate in tandem, they propel the individual and the business into an orbit of high performance.

What are these four pillars?

1. Focus
2. Alignment
3. Delivery
4. Ownership

These four when taken together develop that force which can smash through all obstacles including within.

They create a positive force within the team by which the team is always hunting for opportunities for growth and delivers it.

It makes an individual operate at full potential and beyond in an effortless manner.

I am sharing you this system which is used by all big and successful businesses.

Use this system and get the growth that you desire.

If you are struggling to get growth, then, by applying the method outlined in the book, you will reset the mindset of the team and prepare them for the growth you desire.

If you are a growing business and want to 10X your revenues, then, you need a system which resets the current thinking. The current thinking has got you this far but, 10X of the same effort is not going to take you to 10X growth. The system outlined in this book will reset the thinking and create the foundation for the 10X growth you seek.

This system will work only if you don't treat this as just reading material. Use it as a workbook. After every chapter, write down the insights which you have got or your real life examples to which you can relate the material to. Then, write down what is the Action you will take against it? Who will do it and by when? Taking action is the only way you will get the most out of your investment of time and effort.

Use this system, Develop a world class team and beat your competition in the marketplace.

Earn your spot of glory and become a Leader everyone loves to follow.

Want to know how? Read on.

CHAPTER 2

Focus

If I have to distil everything into one word mantra for business success, then, it would be: FOCUS

Focus brings everything which is required for a business to be successful. It galvanizes the organization. It makes sure that every person in the team gets up in the morning and knows exactly what he needs to accomplish that day.

I remember the time when as a Senior Project Lead, I was managing 42 projects at the same time. The next one year was hell!

Initially, there was a lot of excitement about "let thousand flowers bloom" and each one had something to talk about new. But, early on the sales team was struggling with delivering their day job and also the slew of regional and national initiatives. They were ignored as "naysayers".

However, after three months, none of the projects were moving in their timelines and the enthusiasm, in the beginning, had already waned in the first quarterly review. By six months, the projects were seriously delayed, and tempers had started getting frayed.

By three-quarters, some projects were dropped, and the temptation to add something in their place was severely resisted. By the end of the year, the only projects nearer to the 50% line were those who had senior sponsors and the team had kept their eyes focused on that as much as they could.

Compare that to another time when for two quarters we had just one focus "Beat Competition" in one of our lead product segment. Flowing from the identified goal, each one had specific sub-goals and tasks on monthly, weekly and daily tasks.

The organization was galvanized, and everyone knew what exactly they had to do. We had loads of customer visits not only to sell but to understand what exactly drives their business, what did the competitor do well and how could we beat them at their game.

The single-minded focus meant that every conversation in a meeting started with this key No.1 objective and everyone was clear how we were progressing.

The result was obvious: we handsomely beat the target and threw ourselves a party for creating the distance with a key competitor.

What is it about Focus which works?

Our human brain can keep only a certain number of items in the conscious. At any point in time, we can pay attention ONLY to one thing. Even if today's teens seem to be beating this rule (listening to music, playing a game, watching TV, posting pics in between) in each of them, at one time, the brain is giving Attention to only one thing.

Focus helps in using this to your advantage and not a disadvantage. Imagine a reading glass, when tilted at the correct angle to the sun, can burn paper. This is what Focus brings to the table: Concentration. Have you noticed that when you are fully concentrated on something, you can achieve a lot? For some of us, who come to the office before anybody, why do we achieve a lot? Because there are no distractions; the flip side of Focus.

Focus also brings in clarity. By aiming for one thing, each one knows what the other does, how each of the parts fits with each other Focus brings alignment. As everyone is reaching for the same goal, all efforts and energies are directed to one place. You can wake up someone in the dead of the night and ask them, and they should be able to tell you in one line what the overall aim is.

HOW TO BUILD FOCUS?

Our natural ability of the mind is to be distracted. But, we also have the skill to be focused. Notice I am using the word SKILL. So this needs to be sharpened and trained repeatedly. It is also perishable. So you need to keep working at it.

Whether working as Individuals or Teams, the first question to ask is "What is our overall goal?" This should be in numbers and not "most loved company" (actually, even the second one can be in numbers but not worth its weight in gold as No 1 goal). Let's say it is "x no of sales" So next question: what will get that x no of sales? Y number of customers buying Z number of times.

So now you have an overall goal and beneath that you have two numbers which the entire organization can get focused on delivering it. That's it!

You might say that is too simple. I need more. Sure, add a profit figure. You could add a market share number. But that's it. You don't want to go beyond this. Each figure should be related to the next to make sure they are not different and start driving people in a different direction.

Hey, what about Customer Satisfaction? Sure, that is the very reason your business is in existence. You need to generate 100% satisfaction and pure delight. There is no number to it and it cannot be lower than that.

What about 100k brand ambassadors? Sure, does it lead to Y number of customers buying Z number of times? Then, they are a way to get to the sales number. If not, then it is someone's pet project. The purpose of the brand ambassador has to generate excitement around the brand and develop the attributes you desire for the brand.

But, in the end, it has to generate sales.

What about 10 million customer transactions? Does it lead to Y number of customers buying Z number of times? Then, they are a way to get to the sales number. If not, then it is someone's idea of increasing the value of the business so that you can go into the next round of funding.

Keep chipping away till you make everyone focus on a single number.

What if someone says "I don't come to the office every morning for a number? I come for a higher purpose. To create experiences for customers, to solve their problems". That is motivation, and it's good to keep a picture of the customer on the desk to remind you what drives the business. But, is the picture going to deliver the numbers? It is taking action to delight the customer which results in Y number of customers buying Z number of times.

So keep separating the how from the what. The Goal is the *WHAT*. HOW is the attitude, behavior and the emotions you bring to the job to deliver the *WHAT*. You want passionate, committed and authentic people in your team.

Focus on the Goal as a sniper does. One shot at a time.

To build Focus, we have decided on a Goal.

Now we need to know which of the systems which we use in every division generates the best results.

Checklist for building Focus:

☐   What are the three items (products or services): which make up 70% or more of our Profits?

☐   What are the 2-3 innovations which have successfully passed all the stage gates and have the best promise of delivering their goals in next 1-3 years?

☐   Which marketing programs generate the maximum intention to purchase?

☐   Which production systems generate the best efficiency and quality output?

☐   Which logistics systems deliver my cost and on time in full delivery standards?

☐   Which sales and distribution channels deliver 70% or more of my sales?

Checklist for Focus (continued)

☐   Which sales systems deliver (in person, telecall, online) 70% or more of my sales?

☐   Which Post purchase systems (RM mailers, Email opt-ins, Social media shares) generate the maximum referrals from customers?

☐   Which HR practices delivers the most employee engagement?

☐   Which finance practices and systems deliver the best results?

CHAPTER 3

Alignment

Heavy word but packs the punch. If your team is not aligned to what you want from the business, then you have no hope in hell that you will reach your goal let alone accelerate your business.

So what does it mean? It is the complete, wholehearted commitment to the process and agreed goal.

The best way to know you have it is tragically when you don't have it. If a problem arises and you find someone saying "I told you so" you know, there was nonalignment.

When a plan is laid out, it is expected that people will have differences with where they want to go as well as how they want to go there.

Remember the last family outing you planned and how everyone had a different opinion? Now imagine in your organization. Getting a diverse set of people with their motivations, hopes, and desires to commit and align to a goal and process.

However, no success will happen unless there is total alignment in the team. While I personally prefer 'Just starting ' vs. spending Endless hours trying to create the perfect plan, I do believe that spending time on aligning people on the goal and process is vital.

Often the task of building alignment is almost complete if the right approach is used when Goals are set. What does this mean? If the Goals are Top Down and thrust on the organization, then you will find it way difficult to align everyone to them.

It is when the goals are shared, especially when creating it, then everyone is part of the journey. They don't need to buy in the end as they were part of the process all along.

How to do this? I will shortly explain it.

For now, let's be absolutely clear what alignment means and get it into the very core of the organization.

Why so? Often Agreement masquerades as Alignment. In a meeting, often when all the hidden agendas are not brought out to the table, and people just nod their heads, they are in agreement and not in alignment. Then, when the crunch comes your team will desert you or, to avoid bad news keep hiding the core problem. It will fester and become a much larger problem.

So what is the difference between Agreement and alignment? Why should it matter? You would have seen in countless movies that in the armed forces after every briefing, soldiers are always asked "Any doubts?" this is the final opportunity for the task force to bring their doubts and clarifications on the table.

In business, for various reasons, people tend to keep away their strongest doubts away and "go with the flow". This happens especially if the leader is a very strong personality and does not take no for an answer.

While you want a team committed to the success of the organization, you also want them to commit fully when the action starts. This is where you want full alignment from the team.

So how to build this alignment? Let's see now.

How to build alignment?

A)   Alignment by Goal setting

You want to have a session where you arrive at a goal, either by consensus or you setting the goal. Then ask everyone to see the possibility of the goal. What does it mean for the organization? How will it feel when your team achieves it? Will they be proud explaining to their families and community? Is there more that can be done? The idea is to come with a vivid picture of the goal that you are aiming for and not just a number.

Now get all the critics out and ask what can go wrong? What would make them not aligned to it? This will ensure that all legitimate criticisms and doubts and anxieties are on the table. Ask how can that be addressed?

What needs to be done so that the issues are addressed, without changing the excitement of the goal?

Statements like "this does not happen here" "our industry is not ready for this" "we have never experienced this kind of growth" are to be probed for what is the sentiment behind that. If there is a concern for the company, it needs to be noted and addressed. If it is just plain fear and cussedness, it should be shot down there itself.

Get behind the process next. The process of communicating and aligning the next level and the entire organization. Let the team decide on the exact process of how to achieve the goal. This will make sure that there is buy-in not only to the "What" but also to the "How".

B) Alignment by Behavior reset

Sometimes merely having goals does not mean that people will align. They may have fundamental misgivings about the direction of the company or who is representing them or guiding them.

What are the symptoms of this?

If you are sitting in meetings and along with excuses for non-performance, you also hear teams say

"I thought they wanted it this way." or

"Last quarter sales were prioritizing this item, and suddenly they changed the priority, this time, leading to this disruption."

"Marketing promised us more outdoor support and in-store branding, but it did not arrive in the quantum agreed."

"Finance cleared the X inventory for promotion and one week before we were going to start, we were told to call off the promotion."

"Procurement had promised us that the critical part X will come in the month of May, but it came in the last week of May by which time we had to reschedule our batch orders."

These are more deadly forms. Why so?

They are not open disagreements or non-cooperation between teams. However, something is falling between the gaps, and there is no one to signal that it has happened.

Large organizations, sometimes, respond by having a separate team doing the act of bridge between two departments. e.g. Shopper marketing becomes a bridge between sales and marketing instead of being laser focused on driving category sales in outlets.

This often leads to unnecessary bureaucracy, and you want to avoid it all costs.

So what is the way out?

It is Alignment by Behavior reset. Top management leads it and then cascades below.

Sometimes your senior management team may have great bonhomie but due to the daily practices of the departments, there might be friction in interdepartmental relations.

You start by bringing two departmental heads who have to work together and initiate the process.

These are the questions that they need to answer:

1.   Imagine what would it be like to have perfect alignment within our teams? What values would they display? e.g. Trust, collaboration, openness.

2.   How would they behave on a daily basis? This lays down the ways by which you would evaluate whether there is alignment or not.

3.   What would they think about each other? e.g. "they got my back" "I can totally depend on them" "they are the best team we are working with" This is critical because our thoughts are the voices of our beliefs.

4.   How would they review the level of alignment and know it is working? e.g. monthly or quarterly reviews between team leaders.

Questions for Alignment (continued)

5.   What benefits would it bring to the organization when this happens? This for the heads to realize the real tangible benefits it brings.

6.   How would the teams feel when this level of alignment is present? This is to hardwire the emotions which will eventually drive successful alignment behaviors.

7.   What can go wrong with this alignment? e.g. taking each other for granted, drop in business results in one month

8.   How will it be tackled and who will lead it? e.g. will the teams bring this up on their own or will the departmental heads get together?

9.   How will this alignment level be cemented and raised every year? What is the plan for raising it to every higher level?

Some of these questions may seem unnecessary analysis or "soft", but they are highly important to build the level of alignment which you see in high performing sports teams.

A lot of us move around with assumptions about others and how they are behaving with us.

It is only when we bring out those assumptions in the open then we realize that the other person is a unique human being and is operating with assumptions which may be perfectly legit. But together they create a clash.

Trust me this single step will create a massive silent force inside the organization which when harnessed will speed up your success.

The number one factor which makes teams operate with speed is Alignment.

Once you know that the Team is fully aligned, Move out of the way. No doubts post that. Full steam ahead.

CHAPTER 4

Delivery Mindset

Have you sat in meetings where people go on endlessly discussing and at the end of it, you wonder, what did we achieve? I have.

So what happens? Often in the need to be fully expressed and to get everyone's buy-in, meetings land up with everyone nitpicking.

The point and counterpoint land up becoming positions on which people stake their future if not their lives.

The simple test to check and arrest this, is always to ask "Have we closed this discussion with a decision? Who will be doing what, to deliver what and by when?"

This question, often, brings the conversation to a close and makes sure everyone is clear about what someone had to do and by what time.

By having this mindset, you are also building a delivery mindset in your team.

It is always about getting from Point A to Point B. Once the Point A and Point B are known; we decide how and who does it. This is the most basic template of any business discussion.

Delivery mindset presupposes a No distraction mindset. Let me show you how:

Suppose Joe and Bill (both sales people from different companies) are going from one city to another (separately). Both stop at the same diner to eat. Both get served food which has gone bad.

Joe hollers and screams and calls the manager, they have an argument, Joe screams he will take them to court and resumes his journey and lands up one hour late. The customer is furious that he is late, and the sales call is wasted. Joe blames the diner for ruining his day.

Bill points out the food has gone bad, leaves, buys a sandwich on the go and resumes his journey and reaches on time to conclude his business.

What is the difference?

It is the Delivery no distraction mindset.

Joe forgot that his objective is to reach the meeting on time and food is necessary but not the primary objective. Bill was focused on getting to the meeting.

A Delivery mindset which seeks to accomplish the task/ goal/ project at hand does not allow distractions to disturb the attention. It is focused on the task.

This "must-do" "must-close" mindset leads to the team accomplishing what they have set out to do. Over time, they build the confidence and the history of achieving what they have set out to do. They become the "winning" team, and soon people call them "Lucky."

It is the will and the persistence to close things and the belief that whatever you have set out to do, you must accomplish, which builds and sustains this delivery mindset.

How to build the Delivery Mindset?

I am tempted to say that either you have it or you don't.

But from my experience, it is a skill which can be built.

First off, you need to demonstrate it personally in your behavior. Always ask the question "What will be achieved by this?" before you start anything: a discussion, a meeting, an innovation stage gate call or a sales visit. Then, check after the session is over "Did we achieve what we had set out at the start?" This keeps everyone in the team focused on delivering on what is promised at the start.

This leads to the next behavior i.e. No distractions. Whenever the meeting or the conversation starts straying away from the main objective, refocus.

Ask "Is this in line with what we have set out to do? Or are we moving away from our core discussion?" Always check the relevance of what is being discussed or done with the objective. This leads to the team gradually moving away from distractions and focus on delivery.

You need to show a "whatever it takes" behavior. You need to show how there is a difference between Doing and Trying. This is critical.

You must focus your team on getting things done. If the team is *trying* to achieve results, then, it will not get anywhere.

If they are in a "whatever it takes" zone, they will find a way to get things done.

I remember a time when a critical retailer in my sales channel had his store completely damaged due to rains. We hired a nearby vacant lot and got his team to start selling from there so that there is minimal disruption to his sales. The option of "my biggest customer has his sales washed out so we can't achieve our numbers" was not there. You have to get the "Do whatever it takes" mentality in the team.

Lastly, you need to show how to close discussions, close sales and close every project that is undertaken. Critical to the Delivery mindset is the ability to close.

Some people can never close whether the discussion they are in or the sales call or the project they are in. You have to nudge, prod or hustle and show the team that the business moves only when you close – your discussion, your project or your sales call.

Before someone starts off with a different discussion in a conversation or a project, Ask "Have we closed this conversation (or project)? What have we decided? Who does what? By when?" Your focus on closing conversations will rub off on your team, and they will also get into this delivery mindset.

Is there a difference in being result focused and delivery mindset?

Old Supply chain hands would remember a term which was often used "On time In Full."

Imagine a steeplechase where athletes run and jump across obstacles. Having delivery mindset means not only completing the race but also moving smoothly over the obstacles. Results focused is finishing the race but probably landing in water and hitting an obstacle in the process.

Delivery mindset takes into account both the process as well as the end. However, it operates from the highest "do whatever it takes" and "no distraction" objective.

What would it mean for the various functions within your business?

Checklist for Delivery Mindset:

☐	Portfolio Management: Managing the list of products and services you offer to the Customers. What did we promise ourselves at the start of the year: what milestones in sales and profits do the goods and services need to reach for them to continue, refresh or stop? What actions have we taken against it? Which products and services have we decided to stop, which to continue and which to refresh?

☐	Which of the Top three innovations will we continue and which have we stopped? What learnings have we taken from the innovation to make our pipeline better in the next year?

☐	Which marketing programs will we continue, which we will refresh and which will we stop? What is the decision metrics based on which these decisions are made?

Checklist for Delivery Mindset (continued)

☐ There are two kinds of marketing programs: those which create customers and those which don't. Do we know which ones are which? Have we stopped the ones which don't create customers? How do we accelerate those which do create?

☐ Which production systems (factories, shop floors, assembly lines, own vs. 3rd party) have delivered and which have not? What is the plan to close down the ones which are not delivering consistently over the years?

☐ Which logistics systems are delivering the best response to customer needs? What needs to be done to those which are not? By when will the action be taken and by whom?

Checklist for Delivery Mindset (continued)

☐ What service delivery systems are getting the best customer response? How can they be increased more this year?

☐ What was the service coverage ratio for the distribution system last year? What was the planned increase? Did it happen? What actions helped it? How can we do more of it this year?

☐ Which sales systems (in person, telecall, online) had the best funnel effect (cold prospect – hot prospect – sales call – close)? How do we accelerate it? Which ones do we close or minimize or outsource?

☐ How is the Customer Service delivered and monitored? Is it showing a rising trend of satisfaction? What actions are driving it?

Checklist for Delivery Mindset (continued)

☐ Have we delivered on our promised to our teams and our people? What actions and programs are completed to deliver the maximum engagement?

☐ Are the Financial statements delivered on time and with all statutory compliance in place? How much deviation is present in the working capital management and is it within norms? What actions are driving it? Have we delivered on our BCP plans and actions? Are the Decision support systems easy and effective? Are they available at the point where it has maximum effectiveness?

☐ How much uptime have we delivered in our IT norms? What actions are taken for system security and stability? What actions are taken along with Marketing and Sales to improve data management and more importantly, actioning the insights generated from the data?

CHAPTER 5

Ownership Mindset

You are the leader of the business and the team, and hence, you obviously own the results. And everything which happens between now and the results.

But, does your team own the business?

Why does this matter? If you are an entrepreneur, you will know what I mean.

When your employees are coming to the office or doing their job to collect the paycheck, there is a serious problem. If the job involves a vehicle to get a "bigger" or "better paying" job somewhere else, then there is a problem. When someone says "I just follow instructions. If something goes wrong, it's my boss' problem" there is a serious problem.

When you own the business as if it is your own, you don't wait for instructions. You are always on the lookout for opportunities. You will always want to be one step away and ahead of the competition. You will be the first one to knock on the customers doors. You will be out where it is required to see how your consumers taste and preferences are changing. You will be the "brand ambassador" for your company even if you may be the back office person in the office.

Ownership mindset is the rocket fuel in your business' success. Inspire your team to own the business. Help them see the business as if they are an entrepreneur. Inspire them to go beyond the limitations they have set for themselves. Make them treat the business as if they run the business.

This ownership mindset will make them see every decision as something which either adds value to the business or not.

Then, whether it is giving this discount to the customer or not, or to make the production run for this product or the other, to run the campaign for this product or not, the ownership mindset will show them the right direction.

How to build the ownership mindset?

The first step is in hiring the right people. You want individuals who are curious. Who are looking to better themselves and things around them. Who are asking "how does this add value to the customer?"

Once the team is in, you want to bring Focus on what is most important for you and the business. Make sure they are clear of the One Thing they need to be focused on. The One Thing which is critical for business success.

Once the team is fully aligned and working towards one goal, give them the freedom to achieve their goals. Make them focused on outcomes and delivery.

Be the example of how to avoid distractions and be focused on delivery.

Communicate frequently on what is most important for the business. Make them accountable for their decisions. Celebrate where they have taken decisions which help the business. Celebrate cost consciousness (the no.1 indicator of ownership mindset). Celebrate customer focus and helping customers win their game.

Lead by example.

People will be motivated by your zeal and direction and will start owning the business. Then, you know that many eyes are scanning, identifying and grabbing the opportunities which are always there for the business to grow.

Checklist for the Ownership Mindset:

☐ Have we listed the behaviors which display an ownership mindset?

☐ Are they part of our recruitment questionnaire? What evidence, for the behaviors, are we asking in the interviews?

☐ Are our people asking "how does this add value to the customer?" What actions are they taking based on this question?

☐ What is the one thing which will make the most significant and positive impact on our business? Are we doing it? When? Who is doing it?

☐ What is the one thing which will make the most significant and positive impact on our business TODAY? Are we doing it?

Checklist for the Ownership Mindset (continued)

☐ Which priorities/projects have the maximum positive impact on the business?

☐ How are we allocating our time? What items get the most attention? Are they adding value to the business? How do we stay away from distractions?

☐ What are the key points we need to communicate on this mindset? What behaviors will we give as examples?

☐ What are the ways by which we will celebrate these behaviors in our team?

Checklist for the Ownership Mindset (continued)

☐ What has the team promised and have they delivered them? How do we hold them accountable for their promises? What is our feedback system beyond the performance appraisal system?

☐ How do I hold myself accountable for my promises?

☐ Who has over delivered to our customers? How do we recognize these team members? How do we celebrate this customer focus?

CHAPTER 6

Leadership

Leadership is a big topic, and numerous books are written on it.

The purpose of this chapter is to highlight the Leadership style you need to adopt in the context of the mindset discussion we had.

Here are the aspects of Leadership which you need to be aware of in your style:

SITUATIONAL

Let's be clear about one thing. You are going to unleash Change. As you wade your way through the business implementing and bringing to life the mindset change, this will be a big change for people – in the way they think and behave.

There are many leadership styles and the one most suited for implementing this change program is Situational Leadership Style.

What does this mean?

It means depending on the situation, the task and team at hand you will move from Inspirational to Collaborative to Instructional.

First, you need to dig deep inside yourself and answer for yourself why are you making this change? Sure it is to increase your business and grow. But what does it mean to you personally? What does it mean to your family? What would it mean for your employees? What would it mean to all your partners?

This is not just about money. The increase in business means more jobs in the local community. This means you are increasing abundance and security in the local community.

Your increased business means that your supplier partners may hire more people or do more business with their partners. This means you are increasing the circle of abundance for many more people.

It would mean more bargaining power across various players. This would translate into more profits. This again would mean you will have more funds to invest in your business creating a virtuous cycle.

Or you may want to share the increased profits amongst your employees and yourself. This brings more abundance in your and their lives. This helps them come closer to their dreams: maybe a new house, a dream vacation or could be just a meal in a fancy restaurant which someone had no access to.

Dig deeper into what would your and your team's life be with the increased business.

Paint this vivid picture of the future. What do you see in it?

Now tell your team that this is the meaning that you want for them and yourself. This will help them connect deeper with the change that you are going to implement. This stage requires you to be Inspirational.

When you start implementing the mindset changes, and you are shaping the behaviors esp. on Alignment, you want to be Collaborative.

You want people to express themselves fully. You want all options on the table. You want to make sure that everyone in the team has said what they want to. Here you need to probe gently, listen a lot and encourage everyone to be collaborative. This will help build a team which walks the mile for the other person in the team. It also makes sure that they fully trust each other now that they are fully expressed.

You need to wear the kid gloves to handle them and nudge them in the right direction. You are a bit like a Trek leader.

Carrying everyone together while always keeping the end in sight.

There will be times when there will be confrontations. People will move away from the behaviors that you seek from them. Here you want to be Instructional.

You want to make sure that everyone understands that there are no exceptions to team behaviors and the mindset that you have outlined.

When you find your team looking to you for answers, be clear about what you want and especially your expectations from them. This is not the time to say "You tell me" This is the time you need to be Instructional because that is what they want from you.

Be aware of the situation and tailor your style accordingly.

IMPACT OF YOUR LEADERSHIP

Another area you need to be aware and is related to the Situational Leadership style is the Impact you are having on people.

As a leader of the business and the team, people are always watching you. What are they watching? Your actions.

It's not what you say which is important. It is what you do which is far more important.

Be watchful of how you are presenting the facts, how do you behave in meetings and especially in the informal get-togethers. Some of the things people will watch are:

How do you behave with your immediate reportees? Are you supportive of them? e.g. what happens when your Finance Head says something and your

Sales head opposes it? What do you do? Do you take sides? If yes, whose? If not, then what do you do?

How do you spend the business money? Do you travel coach or business? What does the rest of the team travel?

How much do you tip in a restaurant? Who orders when you are in a restaurant with the team? You or someone else? What happens when someone in the team does not want what someone else has ordered?

What happens when someone escalates a problem to HR or some other departmental head? Do you step in? If not, what happens?

What do you do in a sales visit? Are you in front or behind, when meeting the customer? Do you give the extra budget which the sale person asks for or do you tell him you will get back?

These are just illustrations of formal and informal settings.

I am just giving you a flavor of the myriad situations when someone is watching you.

The good news is that as a leader of the business, people are looking to you for inspiration and following your habits. At least, they will conclude that this is the way how it actually works.

This does not mean you become ultra-conscious of even lifting your pen and get frozen in what others are thinking.

It does mean being aware that this is the impact I am having and this is the way I will communicate what is important to me and what is not.

By being aware of whether what you are doing is in sync with what you are saying, you have the upper hand.

BIAS FOR ACTION

Since we have embarked on a change process, the biggest resistance you will face is Inertia. The love for Status Quo. The "If it isn't broke, don't fix it" mentality.

More simply, everyone is in their comfort zone, and your role is to shake them out of it. Shaken and Fully Stirred.

Perforce this means that your Leadership style must have a Bias for Action.

While you need to give enough space to everyone on whatever they need to contemplate on, through the focus on Delivery Mindset, you need to goad and hustle the team towards action.

What can be done tomorrow needs to be done today. What needs to be done by day end can be finished by afternoon.

Inculcate the habit of starting and completing the most important tasks and priorities at the start of the day. This single habit will create a momentum in your life which will be unstoppable.

COACH NOT TASKMASTER

It must be clear from the Situational Leadership that in the various stages of this change process, you need to wear multiple hats of Leadership.

The common hat through this is that of a coach.

In any sports, you must have watched how the Coach is always watching from the sidelines and sometimes shouting specific instructions. What he is always doing is watching the play as an outsider. He is always watching the game as a dynamic entity.

How is each of the players and in combination affecting the game? What moves is the competition making? Who are the individuals to watch out? Which are the combinations to watch out for? When should one allow the players to play their rehearsed game and when should one come in and guide?

You get the picture.

You have to wear the same hat. Watch how the change process is finding its way across the organization. Who is supporting it? Who is resisting it? How is the change process affecting your suppliers and customers? Which departments are moving with the ball? Which are not moving?

Throughout your eyes and ears must be close to the ground. You must continuously scan the business. You must hear the unsaid words of the team. You must feel their enthusiasm and frustrations with the change process.

Most importantly, you must always be present, guiding them, hustling them if required, in the direction of realizing their full potential and beyond.

AUTHENTIC

People want to see you as an authentic leader. Authentic. The one real quality which everyone desires in leadership.

There has to be perfect congruence between what you say and what you do. By following the "what you see is what you get" style, people learn to trust you and will follow you without hesitation.

You want this trust because once you shift gears to making the organization high performing, you want everyone focused on their deliverables and not second guessing their leaders, particularly not you.

The best way to be Authentic is to keep your promises. People will remember the small things that you do. If you have promised a sales visit after three months, call after three months and do it. If you have promised to visit your factory every two months, then, do it. This predictability of your stated intentions and your behavior builds trust.

Be Authentic and you will have many followers who will walk with you till the end of the earth if required.

CHAPTER 7

Bringing it all Together

By now we have looked at each of the four pillars in detail. We have immersed ourselves in each of the pillars and know the exact steps by which we will build the pillar.

Now, we need to take a step back and get a perspective in how we should bring all of this together. We need to be clear of how all of this will come together. Only then they will be four pillars which together will build the winning mindset.

Here is a checklist for the same:

☐   How would you build this mindset in your business? What industry specific and business specific actions will you take to make this a reality?

☐   How would you build each of the pillars in the team?

☐   How will you personally demonstrate this mindset in you so that you become the inspiration for your team?

☐   How will you role-model this behavior and also in others so that there are more people spreading this message in the organization?

☐   How will you reward these behaviors so that they are entrenched in the organization?

☐   How will you handle objections and rejections to this change process?

☐   How will you connect improving business results to these mindset changes?

☐   What systems will you embed in the organization so that this becomes part of the DNA of the organization?

☐   How will you make sure that new people who join the organization will be inspired to follow this mindset, the same way when you started the change process?

☐   How will you coach yourself to improve continuously on each of these mindsets?

CHAPTER 8

Epilogue

So, is the job done by developing this mindset?

It is just getting started.

Having this mindset is critical to business success but, it needs to be sustained and nurtured. You need to review it every time you meet someone in your business. Is the person demonstrating these behaviors? Then they need to be recognized and celebrating.

In my team outings, formally once a month, when we used to shoot pool or go bowling, I used to reserve one toast always for a team member who had displayed the desired behavior.

It was a way of celebrating a mindset and also to reinforce it in the team. Also, this makes sure that you celebrate periodically so that this becomes a habit in the team. We are quick to criticize but slow in celebrating good behavior and success.

Maybe your way is to take your senior team to an Offsite at an exotic location.

You will have your own ways of celebrating and recognizing. But, you must have one.

Be sensitive to how your people are handling the change. If you have invested the time and energy in developing the winning mindset, they will reward you with their commitment and followership.

Once the how-to-think is taken care of, then the process of How-to-do becomes easier.

Once the foundation with the correct mindset is laid down, then, comes the next stage of putting a structure above it. There are various steps within this next stage too.

Each of us has a Growth Rocket, personal and business. We need to realign with our fullest potential, build a foundation and then, accelerate our game. This is the entire Growth Rocket Series. This book was the Reset and building the Mindset.

I will cover the building and accelerating them in separate books in the series.

But for now, Focus on building them and building them well.

Let me know how your journey goes.

The Journey Continues…

A)   *Want to apply these business principles to your personal life?*

Just to say, thank you, for buying this book, we would like to give you the Personal Guidebook 100% Free.

This Personal Guidebook is a printable PDF. It will enable you to take the principles in this book and apply it for growth in your personal life.

Visit the below link address

http://santoshkanekar.com/personal-guidebook

B)   **Please share your excitement**

If you loved the message the book is giving that to build a successful business, you need to build a winning mindset, then,

Please give a favorable review at the place you bought the book. Reviews help other seekers to make an informed choice. *Please recommend your colleagues* and friend also to purchase the book.

C)   Need definitions for terms?

e.g. BCP, Distribution service coverage
Please visit santoshkanekar.com/terms where I will explain some of the technical terms used in the book.

D)   Need more to jumpstart growth and have a Coach at hand?

Sign up with your email id for Growth updates on santoshkanekar.com

Follow me @santosh_kanekar on Twitter

These posts are designed to give various perspectives in business, leadership and personal growth.

Write to growth@santoshkanekar.com for personal consult.

E)   *Want an early view of the next in series?*

Stay tuned at santoshkanekar.com for preview of the next two books in the series.